S0-BOA-475

Safe From Strangers

For Steve & Anne –

Safe From Strangers

Empowering Children,
From Toddlers
to
Teenagers

Gerri Willever

Gerri Willever

Contributing Author
David A. Freyman, Special Agent FBI

Franklin Mason Press
Trenton, New Jersey

Safe From Strangers Copyright © 2003 Gerri Willever. Printed and bound in the United States of America. All rights reserved. No part of this book may be reproduced in any form or by electronic or mechanical means, including information storage and retrieval systems, without permission in writing from the publisher, except by a reviewer, who may quote brief passages in a review. Published by Franklin Mason Press, P.O. Box 3808, Trenton, NJ 08629. First Edition. www.franklinmasonpress.com.

Cover Design by Peri Poloni, Knockout Design
Cameron Park, CA. www.knockoutbooks.com

Franklin Mason Press ISBN 0-9679227-4-7
Library of Congress Control Number 2003103206

Editorial Staff: Marcia Jacobs, Linda Funari, Catherine Funari

10 9 8 7 6 5 4 3

www.franklinmasonpress.com

The information in this book is true and complete to the best of our knowledge. It is offered without guarantee on the part of the author, contributing authors, and Franklin Mason Press. The authors and Franklin Mason Press disclaim all liability in connection with the use of this book.

Acknowledgements

Gerri Willever, Author

I would like to thank all of the people that helped to bring this book to publication: Lisa and Todd Willever for inspiring me to start the project; Sue Pagels for her laughter and encouragement, which kept me focused until the end; Detective Rich Braconi for all of the information he graciously shared with me.

David A. Freyman, Contributing Author

I would like to thank God, for without his love and guidance all these years, I would not be where I am today. To my dear friend, Lisa Willever who took a chance when she replied to my e-mail and forever changed my outlook on one day becoming published and to Gerri Willever for listening to Lisa and allowing me to contribute to such a wonderful project. Finally, I would like to thank my wife, Debbi and our daughter, Alyssa for being the most wonderful things in my life.

In memory of all the children still not found.

To Rick, Blaine, and Rich who first taught me to be aware...GW

To Debbi and Alyssa...DF

About The Author

Gerri Willever

Gerri Willever, a retired elementary teacher of remedial reading and math, resides in Hamilton, New Jersey. She received her BA degree and MA degree in Reading Education from Glassboro State College, New Jersey. Gerri is co-owner of the American Karate Institute and maintains the rank of Black Belt II. She has also been a student of Taiji and Qigong. The school provides the seminars "Street Survival for Women" and "Safe from Strangers" to students of the karate school and to the community.

About The Contributing Author

David A. Freyman

David A. Freyman, a former United States Marine and 1991 Gulf War Veteran, resides in New Jersey. He received his BA degree in Business Management from East Tennessee State University. David is currently a Special Agent in the Federal Bureau of Investigation and is responsible for investigating many types of Cyber Crime.

Table of Contents

Chapter Three........27
What Can I Do?

Kid tip # 11 - Avoid Deserted Or Lonely Areas
Kid tip # 12 - Yell, Yell, and Yell!
Kid tip # 13 - Yell, Run, And Get Help
Kid tip # 14 - You Have The Right To Say "NO!" To A
               Grown-up
Kid tip # 15 - If It Feels Wrong, Then It Probably Is Wrong
Kid tip # 16 - Run In The Opposite Direction A Car Is Going
Kid tip # 17 - Keep Your Personal Information To Yourself
Kid tip # 18 - Never Tell Anyone That You Are Home Alone
Kid tip # 19 - Become A Moving Target
Kid tip # 20 - *Parents,* Every Second Counts

Chapter Four.......39
How Can I Use The Internet Safely?

Kid tip # 21 - Know The Warning Signs Of Internet Risks
Kid tip # 22 - Keep The Computer In A Common Area
Kid tip # 23 - Keep The Lines Of Communication Open
Kid tip # 24 - Install Parental Blocking/Monitoring Software
Kid tip # 25 - Never Arrange A Face-to-Face Meeting

Chapter Five.........45
Where Can I Learn More?

This section is designed to provide parents with many valuable
resources, including books, websites, and organizations.

Notes......53

Introduction

This book is written as a guide for parents and children to prevent a possible abduction by a stranger. While it is a sad truth that most dangers to children come from people they know, such as neighbors, coaches and their parents' adult friends, this book focuses on the dangers posed by strangers. With recent child kidnappings seizing national headlines, parents are becoming increasingly alarmed.

Unfortunately, as children grow the risks to their personal safety increase. Older children spend more time unsupervised and spend an enormous amount of time on the Internet.

We hope that this book will help you establish a safeguard program with your children, whether they are toddlers or teenagers. It is written in simple terms, so that parents and children can read and learn together. While no one can guarantee that any *one* idea will work, this book contains many practical suggestions, which are easy to understand and use.

We suggest that parents review the material and then share methods and strategies applicable and age-appropriate with their children. By working together, you can make your child more aware of the dangers that exist, and how to avoid them for a bright and happy future.

Chapter 1

Who's That Stranger?

Childhood innocence seems to be lost in the fast times of our present society. No longer is it safe to leave doors and windows unlocked, or even to allow children to play safely outdoors. How do we teach our children to be independent and grow up to lead a safe and vigilant life?

We cannot let the heart-breaking news about missing children overtake our lives, but we cannot ignore the risks either. Although it appears the safety of our children is jeopardized in today's world, parents can breathe easier once they know that the statistics show a different picture. And there is much that you can do to increase the odds in favor of your child.

In 1990 the National Incidence Studies on Missing, Abducted, Runaway, and Thrownaway Children In America (NISMART) conducted a study for the Department of Justice. It found that strangers every year make about 114,699 attempted abductions. Based on FBI reports only about 4% are successful. Smaller fractions, about 200-300, are what are called "stereotypical" kidnappings. The child is transported to a distance of 50 or more miles and kept for ransom, or the abductor intends to keep the child permanently. These make up less than 1% of total abductions. The other category of non-family abductions is the legal definition meaning the child is coerced into a building or vehicle more than 20 feet away for the purpose of committing another crime. The largest number of missing kids is runaways and thrownaways, followed by the lost, family abductions and finally the stereotypical kidnappings. Young teenagers and girls are the most common victims. Statistics indicate that a kidnapping, as we have heard much about through the media, is quite unlikely. However, we still must be vigilant and teach our children the skills they need to stay safe.

Kid tip #1

Never Get Close To Or Into A Strange Vehicle

Ask your child what a stranger is and what does he look like. Children tend to define a stranger as someone they do not know. They see them as being mean and scruffy looking, maybe wearing a mask. This is far from the case. Abductors may look normal and dress appropriately. Some are married, and some are single. Some are young, while others are retired. Some prefer boys, and others prefer girls. There seems to be no one common profile of a child abductor. Most are men; only a small percentage of them are women, and they usually work with a male companion. One abductor was known to dress up as if he belonged at a local construction site, complete with tools, charts and hardhat so he could entice teenage boys.

Be open with your child as you discuss strangers. Define a stranger as a person not introduced to them by you. Local police who work with schools in child safety programs use the term "grown-ups." Children should be cautioned not to speak with any grown-up without your knowledge. As children mature, widen the circle of safe grown-ups to include other adults of whom you approve.

Kid tip # 2:

Never Talk To Anyone You Don't Know Without Your Parents' Permission

Kids must understand that not all strangers are bad. Think about your daily activities. How many people do you come in contact with and you don't know their names? Yet, would we consider them all kidnappers? A "good" stranger will talk to you as they go about their job - bus drivers, clerks, and bank tellers. A "bad" stranger will begin talking for no reason and ask inappropriate questions.

Safe From Strangers

Children should not speak to any stranger unless Mom or Dad has approved - BUT - during an attempted abduction, the rules must change. At this time, the only "bad" stranger is the one trying to take them away. And other grown-up *strangers* may be his or her rescuer!

Talk to your child about good strangers and who can be helpful. Point out helpful "strangers." Play a game to see how many good strangers are around. An example of a "good stranger" is other mothers with children, who would most certainly help a child in need.

An abductor may drive by your house often, tricking the child into thinking that he is a new neighbor. Be wary of names on mailboxes or lawn ornaments that a potential abductor could use to get to know your child's name, and then use that to his advantage. He may hang out at playgrounds or around schools, giving the impression that he belongs there, maybe waiting for his own child. Impress on your child not to talk to any grown-up, no matter how friendly the person seems to be, without your permission. Teach your child not to answer questions or become engaged in a conversation with anyone who does not have your approval. The child should simply say, " I can't talk to you," and move away quickly. This seems to be unfriendly, and goes against what we have been encouraged to do all of our lives. Good people are nice, friendly, and do not cause trouble. But the abductor uses his apparent friendliness to gain the confidence of his victims.

Kid tip #3

<u>Strangers Are Not The Only Concern</u>

As parents, we care about our children's safety. You wouldn't be reading this book if you were not genuinely concerned for them. Many parents have spoken to their children about strangers, not getting into cars, etc. However, we have failed to give our children the right to completely protect themselves if we have left out one important fact. We need to be sure our children understand that it is not always a stranger that could be the person ready to harm them.

Sometimes, unfortunately, a family member, a trusted adult friend, or even an older child will want to harm your child. In most families this is unlikely to occur, just as an attempted abduction is statistically not likely to happen. However, kids need to understand that it could happen. We learn many safety skills in our lives: fire safety, first aid, water safety, how to perform CPR. Most of us never have to use these skills, but we are glad to know what to do if that emergency should occur. These are the same type of safety skills. Your child will probably never need them, but they are good to know.

No one has the right to touch your child in any way that makes him or her feel uncomfortable or confused. This rule is for any age child from the very young to the older teenager. No one should be touching him or her in any place that is covered by a bathing suit. People who like to do that are called pedophiles. Sometimes, pedophiles prey on family members, and these people are much more subtle about getting the child to cooperate. All of the rules about strangers apply. Children need to tell another adult quickly.

Kid Tip # 4:

You Don't Have To Keep A Secret If It Makes You Uncomfortable

Oftentimes, a family member or family friend will try to frighten a child by saying that he will hurt another family member, or use some other mean tactic to make a child keep the abuse a secret. This is a trap and it is important for children to tell someone right away that they are being hurt.

Many times parents don't want to believe such a thing could happen. They cannot understand how someone they have trusted could possibly do such a thing. But we as parents must believe our children and children should be taught to keep telling trusted grown-ups until they find an adult to listen and to help.

Be watchful of a strong bond forming between your child and any adult. Is that person showering lots of attention on your child? No one should be paying more attention to your child than you. Parents need to be on the alert if a child suddenly behaves differently. This may be a sign that something serious is happening and he or she does not know how to handle it.

The more you talk with your child and spend quality time together, the easier it will be for him or her to approach you before something really bad happens. Keep an open dialogue with your child and encourage her/him to tell you if anyone makes them feel uncomfortable. That's hard to do these days when there are so many family activities going on, but the end result is worth the time and effort.

You need to educate your child about the possibilities much as you would teach them about being safe in other daily activities. They need to be aware, but not paranoid. You want to give them a sense of empowerment about their safety, rather than a sense of helplessness. Teach them that they can be strong and make safe choices.

Safe From Strangers

Chapter 2

What's Around Me ?

One of the first things that children, as well as adults, need to learn to do is to become more familiar with their surroundings and to be more observant. This is especially true when in familiar places, which are often frequented. Children, and adults, become complacent because they're in a safe, familiar environment, such as the neighborhood, the front yard, or a favorite play area. They become engrossed with an activity and do not notice what or who is around. It has always been safe so no one thinks about staying alert. But 80% of abductions happen less than one quarter of a mile from the last known location of the victim. And 65% are less than 200 feet from the victim's own home.

Being aware means feeling relaxed where you are, but still mindful of your environment. Visually scan the surroundings. Where is the safest place to go if you had to get out of danger? Look for threatening behaviors of people and situations. Are there any strange cars going by? How close is that stranger to you? Is he watching you and your friends or approaching you? How can you avoid that person? Are there any safe strangers nearby, like a mother with her children, or the mailman? What are other people around you doing? Is a grown-up trying to be overly friendly with children or asking them for help? These are all little clues to be keeping in mind.

Kid Tip #5

Grown-ups Don't Ask Kids For Help

If an honest, responsible adult needs help, then he will seek help from another adult, not a child. Telling children not to talk to a stranger is not enough. You need to give them options. Be honest and tell them why and who not to speak with. They should not be talking to anyone who has not been introduced to them by a parent.

Children should beware of questions an abductor might use to trick them, "Hey, how do I get to Main Street?" or "Can you help me find my puppy?"

Kid Tip #6

You Don't Have To Answer A Grown-up's Question If You Don't Want To

Most muggers or burglars select their victims carefully before the attack. If a house is alarmed and secured, a burglar may move on. If people have a confident appearance about themselves, the mugger will not choose to rob that person. Kidnappers do the same. They search for an easy target. They usually do not attack a child in a group. They look for one that is alone or too trusting. Most try to trick a child into coming complacently. They do not want any attention drawn to themselves, and they want to leave quickly.

Kid Tip #7

There's Safety In Numbers

Kids should know where the exits are in a public place. They should locate the check-out counters in stores which are safe places to go. Take a walking tour with your child to places you oftentimes visit. Identify areas to go for help. Look around for good strangers that could help in an emergency. Caution your child to never, under any circumstances, leave a store if they have become separated from you.

They should be taught to stay near the front of the store. Never let anyone take them to the back of a store, even if they are told that their parent is there waiting for them. A child should stay at a counter or safe place until their parent is brought to them.

Mutually determine a safe meeting area in each store should you inadvertently become separated. Parents, never lose sight of your children. Kids, don't wander away from your parent. Be sure that you can see each other at all times.

Impress on your child not to go with anyone. If a stranger says there is an emergency at home, the child should respond with, "No, I can't go with you." Keep a distance from the stranger at all times.

Kid tip # 8

Have A Special Code Word Known Only To You And Your Parents

Some families have a secret code word known only within the family. Before your child goes with anyone other than his or her parents, the code word must be used. For instance, if a neighbor shows up at the park and informs your child that he is to bring him or her home, a code word will let your child know that you have sent him. It is a good idea to change the word if it has been used. This assures that others have not overheard the word accidentally. Children should not share the word with anyone. Some abductors are sly and use the child's fear to get them to say the word. If your child thinks that there is an emergency, encourage her/him to ask for a marked police car. A potential abductor will not stick around!

Kid tip #9

When In Doubt, Trust Your Instincts

Abductors are skillful in getting young children to talk to them even when the child knows not to do this. One of the most common tricks is to offer the potential victim a treat, or for teens, the lure of an easy job and quick money. He might say something like, "I'm going to McDonald's - do you want a burger?" Remember - if it seems too good to be true, it probably is not true. Some kidnappers ask kids to help them carry packages to their car, or help to look for a really cute, lost puppy, even showing a picture of an adorable looking dog.

Some predators may appear to be ill or injured and in need of serious help. Keep a distance and offer to get help or call for 911. Children should start running away as they make the offer. Don't hang around for his response. If he really needs help, he will wait there. Some criminals even dress as police officers and use the figure of a person in authority to trick kids into trusting them. A police officer in a uniform will probably have a marked police car or motorcycle.

Kid tip# 10

<u>Do Not Allow Anyone Into Your Personal Space</u>

Children not only need to be aware of their surroundings, but also need to be cautious in not letting anyone get too close to them. Abductors are sly and will try to catch their victims off-guard in order to get in close and quickly snatch them. This is why children should be taught to protect their personal space. Have your child stand up and extend his or her leg straight out in front. That's the distance of his or her personal space. That length, plus a little more, depending on the size of the stranger, is a safe distance to keep from someone. A taller person will require a child to stay even farther away than this. Children should not allow anyone into their personal space.

Everyday we allow people into our personal space - family, friends, or teachers. The key word is: **allow**. Children have the right to keep someone out of their space if they are feeling uncomfortable about it.

Chapter 3

What Can I Do?

While the first two chapters are written to the parent, this chapter is devoted to providing children with effective strategies and is written to the child. Parents, teachers, and others involved in a child's growth should work together to develop a child's self-esteem. A child that feels good about himself or herself will be on the way to developing a positive self-image.

Being aware of your environment and your own feelings is a good start down the path of self-protection. Just knowing what or who is around you is not enough, though. You need to display a confident attitude about yourself.

Your body language indicates how confident you are in yourself. A person who slouches, walks with his head down or acts fearful, is showing that he or she is timid, and thus a possible victim. On the other hand, someone who is walking tall and with a purpose, looking straight ahead, and acting in a confident manner, will present the opposite picture to an abductor. This person appears to be one who is apt to make noise or put up a struggle, which would bring attention to the act. Remember, the dangerous stranger does not want any attention focused on him, especially in the act of committing a crime. Don't be afraid to look into the face of a stranger coming too close. He does not want to be identified.

Kid Tip # 11

Avoid Deserted Or Lonely Areas

We often think of self-defense as punching, kicking, or doing cool karate moves. But self-defense is broader than that. It involves doing whatever you need to do to keep yourself safe. That means staying away from rough kids, avoiding places that are unsafe, such as deserted buildings, alleys, and dark streets. If you're not there, you can't be hurt. Don't walk some place alone. Always be with a friend. Self-defense also means using everything you have to defend yourself, and that includes something everyone has, does not require training and is free - it's your voice!

Parents and teachers often tell children to be quiet, and polite and to respect all adults. They tell their kids not to yell. But, when it comes time to yell for help, kids must yell no matter how frightened or embarrassed they may be.
Many children are concerned with the "What ifs." What if he

really wasn't going to hurt me? What will they think of me if I am wrong? What if he really needed help? People might laugh at me if he was not really an abductor. But kids should never be embarrassed to yell if they feel they are in danger. It's better to have screamed for help and have been wrong, than to take that chance. The old adage "Better safe, than sorry," is still true.

Kid Tip #12

<u>YELL, YELL, AND YELL</u>

Many childhood safety experts are now teaching children not to yell "Help," but something else instead. "Fire" is a great attention-getter. When someone yells, "Fire!" it becomes a concern to everyone around, because everyone's safety may be compromised and will look to see what is going on. This is exactly what an abductor does not want. Police and other safety groups are also encouraging children to yell "Stranger!" or "This isn't my Dad!" Whichever you choose, it must be something you are comfortable yelling. Stick to the same word so you are not confused in an emergency.

Your voice must be loud, strong, and assertive. Practice yelling so that it becomes natural to you. It may seem funny or not very cool, but if you have not prepared yourself to yell when you are not in danger, you are less likely to yell if something really happens.

Kid Tip #13

Yell, Run, And Get Help

Kids should know that yelling must take place before the stranger even puts his hands on them. As soon as you get that funny feeling inside, or see something is not right, that's the time to be yelling and run. Run to the safest place. Remember in Chapter 2, you looked around for safe places. If the safe place is in the direction of the stranger, go the other way.

Kid Tip #14

You Have The Right To Say " NO" To A Grown-up

In Chapter 2 we discussed your personal space. Don't allow anyone you don't want into your space. You have the right to yell "STOP!' to an adult if he is approaching you for no reason. If he doesn't stop, broaden the distance between you. Run in the opposite direction. Run in a zigzag pattern. It's much harder for an adult to keep up with you. Listen to your little voice inside of you if something feels wrong. It is OK to run and yell. If you feel threatened do not hesitate to follow your true feelings. You do not have to talk to this person, listen to his problems, or respond in any way. Just get away fast.

Kid Tip #15

If It Feels Wrong, Then It Probably *Is* Wrong

Did you ever do something that you knew you should not be doing and felt uneasy about it? Some people call this a "gut feeling," or their conscience, or a little voice inside of them. It's all the same idea. It's your center, your spirit, protecting you naturally from harm. Listen to that voice or feeling. Begin running and yelling. Don't wait around to see if you are right. Don't question yourself. Child abductors, interviewed from jail, have said that if a victim made noise they left them alone. They do not want attention. No one can guarantee this will work every time, but it's your best chance.

Once you have successfully escaped from an abductor, there are several things you need to do. First and foremost, you must remain calm. Don't panic. Then you must get help. Remember the good strangers? Find one now. Locate a mom, a store clerk, a pedestrian, or a passing motorist.

Bob Stuber, who developed Escape School, and whose website is noted in chapter five, recommends the "Velcro Technique." We are all familiar with the stickiness of Velcro. Grab someone and don't let go (become a piece of

Velcro) as you tell him or her that you have been kidnapped and need help. Do this to any good stranger that you are trying to get help from. Don't leave that place for any reason unless a uniformed police officer has arrived. Do not go with anyone else.

As you are looking for help, keep running and begin drawing attention to yourself to get help fast. It's OK. When everyone realizes what has happened things will calm down.

Kid Tip # 16

Run In The Opposite Direction
A Car Is Going

A common trick of abductors is getting a child close to and then into a car. As mentioned earlier, seemingly innocent questions such as "Where is Main Street?" or "How do I get to the park?" can be an attempt to catch you off guard and to grab you. Be on the alert if a car slows down or begins to follow you. Do not answer any questions, or stay around to listen to his problem. A great tactic is to begin running in the opposite direction that the car is moving. It is much more difficult for the car to turn around, giving you more distance and time to escape.

Kid Tip # 17

<u>Keep Your Personal Information To Yourself</u>

Avoid having your name on clothing or toys where it is visible to everyone. Abductors have used that to their advantage by tricking a child into thinking a stranger is someone who knows the family. "Hey, Karen, your mom asked me to give this to you."

As you are walking to and from school or the bus stop, you are probably toting a backpack, books, or special projects in your hands. If you need to make a run for it, you must be prepared to drop your belongings. Don't be concerned about them. They will only be a hindrance to you as you try to get away. Practice with your family slipping out of your backpack if someone comes from behind and grabs you. Try wiggling out of an adults grasp. Squirm, move about, and don't stop. Be like a cat that does not want to be held. Keep screaming and moving all of the time. This makes it very difficult for an abductor to hold on to you. Run and leave your stuff behind. You can also use your books as a weapon. Throw them at him as you begin to make your escape. Schoolbooks and assignments can be replaced. You, however, cannot be replaced.

Another trick that an abductor uses is to try to pull a child off his or her bike. Your bike could really be a safety tool for you. The Escape School teaches kids how to wrap their arms around the bike and make it more difficult to get you off of it. Simply hug the handlebars and the bike. Hold on tightly. Now the abductor has a bigger problem. Oh yes, and don't forget to yell. If you can get off the bike, get off on the opposite side of where he is, so now the bike is between the two of you. Push it towards him, so he has to move it. This gives you time and space to run away.

Kid Tip #18

Never Tell Anyone That You Are Home Alone

If your parents must leave you at home alone, be sure you know and understand the rules that they have set down. You never tell a caller on the phone that you are home alone. Don't get into a conversation with that person. Tell him/her that mom or dad is busy and will return their call. Role-play with your parents and practice possible answers. Avoid saying that your mother is in the shower. Everyone seems to know that one. Be sure your parents have placed emergency telephone numbers near each phone. Learn about 911 and how it operates. **Most importantly, never hang up while on the phone with 911.**

What Can I Do?

Do not open the door for any reason. This is a good safety rule for everyone in the family. Always ask who it is. If you do not know them, do not open that door. Call 911 or a neighbor if you think something is wrong. Be aware of that uneasy feeling. If grown-ups are expecting deliveries, have them sent to a neighbor's house.

Never invite anyone home with you if you do not have permission from your parents. You cannot be sure who would accidentally tell someone that you are home alone after school.

The safety rules that apply to strangers you might meet on the street or talk to on the phone also apply to strangers on the Internet. The web is a great way to learn, do business, play games, or email friends with just the click of your mouse. However, it can be just as dangerous as meeting a bad stranger on the street. You really don't know anything about someone you meet on the Internet. It's very easy for a predator to give false information on-line. Most strangers, as in our daily lives, are honest and friendly. There are, however, scam artists, criminals and other dangerous people on the web ready to connect to unsuspecting victims.

Chapter Four provides valuable strategies for parents of children who use the Internet.

Kid Tip # 19

Become A Moving Target

Now what if the unthinkable happens. Relax, all is not over yet. You still have things that you can do to get away. Start kicking at his knees. It doesn't take much power to break a knee - only about seven pounds of force - so start kicking hard, not with the toes but the bottom of your foot. If he grabs your arm, Stuber says, be a windmill. Make a big circle with your arm, which will release his grip and then run away in the direction of his back. Don't stay in front of him. Now is the only time that you are allowed to bite anyone. It just might be the trick to make him release you. If you can, poke his eyes.

The natural response of anyone who has been poked in the eye is to reach up for the eye. Just what you want him to do so you can now run and yell. If you should get dragged into a car, stay calm and watch for a time to react. Don't cry and become timid. Keep making a commotion.

Many children are now fearful of an abductor entering the house and taking them from their own bed. Stay calm and fight back. If anything like this should happen, then you must respond in the same manner as if you were outside. Start yelling! Knock stuff off of the dressers or tables in your room. Make a commotion. And make sure your parents have locked all of the doors and windows in your home before going to bed.

Kid Tip # 20

Parents, Every Second Counts

Law enforcement agencies tell us that the most crucial time for an abducted child is within the first hours that a child is missing. As soon as you are aware that your child is gone, you need to call the police immediately. It's a good idea to keep an identity kit of your child. Include a recent frontal picture, height, weight, and fingerprints of your child.

Fingerprint Imaging Services

This innovative company, whose website is mentioned in Chapter Five, has a valuable product called *"Just About Me."* This child identification kit provides parents with the necessary tools to develop a kit for each child in the family. In addition, event coordinators work with local law enforcement agencies and school districts to provide kits and consulting services.

While we are in no way affiliated with this, or any organization mentioned, we feel it is imperative to provide parents with information regarding products that will improve the safety of their children.

Fingerprint Imaging
3730 132nd St. SW
Lynnwood, WA 98037
Toll Free: 1-877-741-3082
http://justaboutme.com

Other websites, in Chapter Five, also have kits available or tell you how to make your own. The key is keeping it up to date.

The Amber Alert System is a voluntary partnership between law enforcement agencies and broadcasting systems. It was created in 1996 in memory of Amber Hagerman, who was abducted and killed in Arlington, Texas. The Dallas/Fort Worth Association of Radio Managers and local law-enforcement agencies teamed up to develop this unique early-warning system to help find abducted children. Since then, more that 28 states have developed an Amber Alert Plan. The Broadcasters utilize The Emergency Alert System, formerly called the Emergency Broadcast System, to initially interrupt programming with an alert. A photo and an alert at the bottom of the television screen will appear, much like when a severe weather emergency appears. Some states are using the alert system on overhead signs on highways.

AmberAlertNow.org is a campaign from the Polly Klaas Foundation, a non-profit organization dedicated to educating the public on child abduction prevention, and aids in the search for missing children. There are many agencies ready to help if something should happen. It is important to act immediately.

Chapter 4

How Can I Use The Internet Safely?

More and more children are being exploited and/or abducted via the use of the Internet each year. The importance of remaining active in our children's everyday lives has become an increasingly important task that we cannot fail.

The Internet is a never-ending source of information and, for the most part, the benefits outweigh the risks for anyone that logs onto the "information super-highway." In order to minimize the risks that are present, parents can apply various strategies to keep their children safe.

The key to Internet safety is quite inexpensive. It is parental involvement during a time when most children expect a certain level of privacy. The following strategies help parents to achieve involvement while respecting their growing children.

Safe From Strangers

For many parents, the Internet has become another form of baby-sitting or a way to keep children occupied while they relax or take care of business. In most instances, the parents succumb to the pressure of a child to place the computer out of sight of the parents. Most of the time the computer ends up in a child's room as this is where most homework is done. But this can be a mistake, even with older children. Parents are less likely to be involved with a child later in the evening, after the homework is complete. And this is the time when a predator is most likely to seek victims.

Another time when a child is most vulnerable to a predator's advances is after school, when a parent is likely to be at, or on their way home from work.

As technology advances, the risks surrounding a child's safety increase also. The annonymity of the Internet creates an environment of easy deception. During the teenage years it is often difficult for children to fit in with a group of peers and many children, without their parents' knowledge, seek on-line friendships.

Often times, when a child is involved in something that may be of a suspicious nature, a parent's intuition kicks into high gear. But all too frequently, parents are unaware of a child's on-line activities during the time when they are otherwise occupied.

Kid Tip # 21

<u>Know The Warning Signs of Internet Risks</u>

Some of the warning signs that a child may be involved in risky on-line activities are as follows:

> 1. Your child dramatically increases the amount of time spent on the Internet, especially late into the night.

> 2. Your child is disinterested in family activities and is short tempered when questioned.

> 3. Your child's schoolwork begins to decline and he or she neglects other responsibilities as well.

> 4. Your child turns the monitor off or switches to a different screen when you enter the room.

> 5. Your child receives packages or unexplained gifts from unknown individuals, which can include clothes, jewelry, or even money.

The only way to truly know what is going on with your child and the Internet is to get involved.

Kid Tip # 22

Keep The Computer In A Common Area

First and foremost, move the computer to a common area so that everyone has access and can be physically monitored at any time. In doing so, the computer becomes a family-oriented activity-center.

As mentioned earlier, a child is more likely to be involved with inappropriate on-line conduct when not being monitored. This frequently happens after school, unless the computer is in a common area. This increases a child's possibility of being observed using the Internet in an inappropriate manner. Most children will be less likely to risk that sort of conduct.

Kid Tip # 23

Keep The Lines Of Communication Open

It is important to talk to your child and find out what is going on in his or her life. Explore the Internet together and allow them to make mistakes in your presence. Doing so will provide parents with an opportunity to explain the dangers that exist and the ease in which one can go astray.

Kid Tip # 24

Install Parental Blocking/Monitoring Software

Search the various computer retail stores for parental blocking programs to prevent many of the unsolicited, sexually explicit materials from being received or viewed by your children. While the software cannot offer a one hundred percent guarantee, it blocks much of the unwanted, explicit web sites.

In addition, you may want to consider placing parental monitoring software on your computer, with your child's knowledge, in order to determine where they have been. This software provides parents with specific information as to the web sites their children are visiting and the chat rooms they enter, which can be helpful if they are abducted.

Take the time to explain to your children the importance of the monitoring software. Let your child know that while you trust him or her; you do not trust strangers on the World Wide Web. Explain to children that on-line strangers are often more dangerous than those they encounter in public. Encourage them to report inappropriate conversations or sites that they encounter. This will create an open environment and the software will be viewed as protection, rather than an invasion of privacy.

Kid Tip # 25

Never Arrange A Face-to-Face Meeting

Finally, tell your children to never arrange face-to-face meetings with anyone they have met on-line. They should never provide any personal information about themselves or their family, such as name, address, telephone number, and/or the school that they are currently attending.

All too often, children are communicating with a predator they believe to be a peer. It is not uncommon for a child to develop high levels of trust with someone they communicate with everyday. Predators will take the time to establish this trust and slowly learn the details of your child's life. Once trust has been established, it becomes quite easy to arrange a meeting. It is imperative to repeatedly discuss the dangers with your child.

> If, for any reason, you feel as though your child has turned up missing or exploited and it involves the Internet, you should immediately call your local police, your local FBI office, and/or the National Center for Missing and Exploited Children at 1-800-843-5678. You can also report the incident at the following National Center for Missing and Exploited Children web site: www.missingkids.com/cybertip.

Chapter 5

Where Can I Learn More?

The following is a collection of Internet web sites, which have additional information to explore with the entire family. Some sites offer techniques and tips for your children; some include health and safety tips for everyone in the family. Other sites will link you to safe places to visit on the web.

Web Sites

http://www.missingkids.com

Official web site for The National Center for Missing and Exploited Children (NCMEC). This is a private non-profit organization co-founded in 1984 by John Walsh. Its mission is to locate missing children, and to raise public awareness of missing and exploited children.
Phone: 1- 800 - The Lost (1-800-843-5678)

Safe From Strangers

http://www.cybertipline.com

A division of NCMEC established for anyone to report information about missing or exploited children.

http://www.justaboutme.com

This innovative company has a valuable product called *"Just About Me."* This child identification kit provides parents with the necessary tools to develop a kit for each child in the family.

http://www.kidzprintz.com

Kidz Printz Child ID kits were originally designed for law enforcement agencies and are now made available for free to families anywhere in North America. The site is simple to use and a very effective tool. It also contains award-winning links about child abduction, safety, health and first-aid for the family.

http://www.escapeschool.com

Provides printable articles about safety tips for the entire family, as well as free presentations to schools and other organizations.

Where Can I Learn More?

http://casakar.clarityconnect.com

A karate school website that teaches children personal safety habits; and it has downloadable safety coloring pages for children.

http://www.enough.org/safeharbors.htm

Offers safe links on the Internet for the entire family.

http://www.familykaratecenter.com/capp.htm

A karate school website which offers safe links for kids and also gives child abduction prevention advice.

http://www.fingerprintamerica.com/parentstips.html

Manufactures and sells child ID fingerprint kits and other safety products for the family; and it has downloadable safety tips for your child.

http://kidalert.net/home.htm

Manufactures and sells child ID kits as well as other safety products and downloadable safety tips.

Safe From Strangers

http://www.yellodyno.com

Non-fearful, musical programs for schools, parents, and other groups about abuse, abduction, date rape, and other risks.

http://maxpages.com/firstdefense

A Parent's Guide to Kidnapping Prevention Website, what to teach a child at different ages, self-defense techniques, and a videotape is available.

http://hendersonville-pd.org

Lists many child abduction prevention tips, as well as other safety ideas.

http://www.klasskids.org

Founded in 1994, this organization dedicates itself to stopping crime against kids; links to other sites available.

http://www.pollyklass.org

A non-profit organization dedicated to educating the public on the prevention of child abductions; the organization also aids in the search of missing children. The site has downloadable safety hints.

Where Can I Learn More?

http://www.AmberAlertNow.org

A campaign from the Polly Klass Foundation working to develop the Amber Alert System in all states.

http://safekids.com

Offers tapes and advice to make your family's online experience fun.

Books

Arrenburg, Gerald S., Carmelia R. Bartimole, and John E. Bartimole, **Preventing Missing Children** - A Parental Guide to Child Security, Compact Books, Inc. 1984

Chalet, Donna, and Francine Russell, The Safe Zone - **A Kid's Guide to Personal Safety**, Morrow Junior Books, New York, 1998

Chalet, Donna, **Staying Safe on the Streets,** The Rosen Publishing Group, Inc. New York, 1995

Chalet, Donna, **Staying Safe at School**,The Rosen Publishing Group, Inc. New york, 1995

Chalet, Donna, **Staying Safe on Dates,** The Rosen Publishing Group, Inc. New York, 1995

Chalet, Donna, **Staying Safe While Traveling**, The Rosen Publishing Group, Inc. New York, 1995

Colao, Flora and Tamar Hosansky, **Your Children Should Know,** The Bobbs-Merrill Co., Inc., Indianapolis/New York, 1983

Goedecker, Christopher J., and Rosemarie Hausherr, **Smart Moves A Kid's Guide to Self-Defense**, Simon & Schuster Books for Young Readers, New York, 1995

Gutman, Bill, **Be Aware of Danger,** Twenty-First Century Books, A Division of Henry Holt Co. Inc. New York, 1996

Wiloch, Thomas, **Everything You Need to Know About Protecting Yourself and Others From Being Abducted**, Rosen Publishing Group, Inc. New York, 1998

<u>OTHER RESOURCES</u>

Center for Child Protection and Family Support
717 G Street, SE
Washington, DC 20003
202-544-3144

National Clearinghouse on Families & Youth
PO Box 13505
Silver Springs, MD 20911-3505
301-608-8098

National School Safety Center
148 Duesenberg Drive, Suite 11
Westlake Village, CA 91362
605-373-9977

Team H.O.P.E.
Help Offering Parents Empowerment
A parent support network for families of missing children
1-800-306-6311

Safe From Strangers

Notes

_____

_____

_____

_____

_____

_____

_____

_____

_____

_____

_____

_____

_____

_____

_____

Who's That Stranger?

_____

_____

_____

_____

_____

_____

_____

_____

_____

_____

_____

_____

_____

_____

_____

_____

_____

_____

_____

_____

_____

_____

_____

_____

_____

_____

_____

_____

_____

_____

_____

_____

_____

Who's That Stranger?

_____

_____

_____

_____

_____

_____

_____

_____

_____

_____

_____

_____

_____

_____

_____

_____

_____

_____

_____

_____

_____

_____

_____

_____

_____

_____

_____

_____

_____

_____

_____

_____

_____

_____

Who's That Stranger?

_____

_____

_____

_____

_____

_____

_____

_____

_____

_____

_____

_____

_____

_____

_____

_____

_____

_____

_____

_____

_____

_____

_____

_____

_____

_____

_____

_____

_____

_____

_____

_____

_____

_____

_____

Who's That Stranger?

_____

_____

_____

_____

_____

_____

_____

_____

_____

_____

_____

_____

_____

_____

_____

_____

_____

Where Can I Learn More?

_____

_____

_____

_____

_____

_____

_____

_____

_____

_____

_____

_____

_____

_____

_____

_____

_____

_____

Who's That Stranger?

_____

_____

_____

_____

_____

_____

_____

_____

_____

_____

_____

_____

_____

_____

_____

_____

_____

_____

_____

_____

_____

_____

_____

_____

_____

_____

_____

_____

_____

_____

_____

_____

_____

_____

_____

Who's That Stranger?